12 Short Hikes
NEAR LAKE PLACID

PLUS The Saranac Lake 6

BY PHIL BROWN

 An ADIRONDACK EXPLORER Guidebook

Mount Van Hoevenberg rewards hikers with a stupendous High Peaks vista.

Published by:
ADIRONDACK EXPLORER
36 Church Street, Saranac Lake, NY 12983
AdirondackExplorer.org
&
LOST POND PRESS
Saranac Lake, NY
LostPondPress.com

Cover Photo: Mount Jo by Nancie Battaglia
Back Cover Photo: Mount Van Hoevenberg by Nancie Battaglia
Book Design: Susan Bibeau

ISBN: 978-0-9903090-0-0

Foreword

We at the *Adirondack Explorer* believe that the Adirondack Park is one of the most beautiful places on the planet. That's why our newsmagazine focuses on ways to protect and enjoy it. We hope this guidebook will lead to adventures that will enhance your appreciation of this marvelous place.

Although I wrote the book, many others had a hand in its production. Susan Bibeau designed the covers and inside pages. Nancy Bernstein drew all the maps by hand. And Lake Placid's Nancie Battaglia provided most of the photographs. We are lucky to have such talented people contributing to every issue of the *Explorer*. I want to thank Tom Woodman, the *Explorer* publisher, and Betsy Dirnberger, the associate publisher, for reading my copy, catching mistakes, and offering helpful suggestions. For moral support, I am grateful to everyone at the *Explorer*, including the publication's founder, Dick Beamish.

If you're unfamiliar with the *Explorer,* please take the time to check it out. We are a nonprofit newsmagazine that publishes six issues a year in addition to an annual Outings Guide. For Adirondack aficionados, it's essential reading. You can request a free issue at **adirondackexplorer.org**.

Enjoy the hikes!

–**Phil Brown**

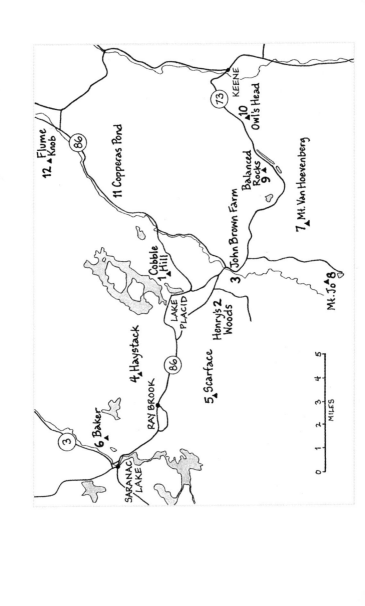

CONTENTS:

Introduction

More than ten thousand people climb Mount Marcy every year, and it's easy to understand why. Marcy has the cachet of being the highest peak in New York State, and its bald summit affords an incomparable panorama of the Adirondacks. But hiking Marcy is a full-day commitment. From Heart Lake, the round-trip to the summit is fifteen miles, with 3,166 feet of elevation gain during the ascent. Not everyone has the time, the desire, or the stamina to undertake such an outing.

This is where *12 Short Hikes Near Lake Placid* comes in. The *Adirondack Explorer* newsmagazine has chosen a dozen relatively easy hikes within ten miles of Lake Placid. If you can hike two miles an hour, any of them can be done in one to four hours. (If you have small children or novice hikers in your group, you may need more time.) Most of the hikes lead to summits or lookouts with views of the High Peaks. We also selected two lowland hikes with impressive views of the region's big mountains.

As a bonus, we added a chapter on climbing the Saranac Lake 6—a half-dozen smallish peaks near the village of Saranac Lake, which is just up the road from Lake Placid. Hikers who climb all six earn a cloth patch that can be sewn onto a backpack or clothing. Three of the six are among the *12 Short Hikes*. The other three hikes were either too far away or too arduous to be included in the main part of the book, but they are described in the Saranac Lake 6 chapter. In all, then, this book details fifteen hikes.

For each outing, we include clear driving directions and GPS coordinates to get you to the trailhead. We provide a statistical overview (distance, elevation gain, etc.) to allow you to gauge the difficulty of the hike. The descriptions of the hikes are concise but informative. We let you know what mountains you're looking at. The trails are shown in the distinctive hand-drawn maps of Nancy Bernstein, a local artist. Most of the photos were shot by Nancie Battaglia, a Lake Placid resident whose work appears in publications all over the world.

Although these are short hikes, don't take them lightly. Whenever you enter the wilderness, you should be prepared in case someone breaks an ankle or worse. This means carrying the **Ten Essentials**. The classic list is as follows: **map, compass, sunglasses and sunscreen, extra clothing, headlamp or flashlight, first-aid kit, fire-starter, matches, knife, and extra food**. It's also wise to carry an emergency shelter such as a space blanket, a lightweight tent, or just a large trash bag. If you have a cell phone, bring it for emergencies, but be aware that it may not pick up a signal in the wild.

Most of these hikes are in the Forest Preserve, public land protected by the state constitution as "forever wild." In some cases, you cross private property and thus should not wander from the trail. Whether you're in the Forest Preserve or on private property, respect the land. Leave it as you found it.

The Adirondack Park contains 2.6 million acres of Forest Preserve, with thousands of miles of trails. We hope hiking the trails in this book will inspire you to discover more of the Adirondacks. If so, you should consider joining the Adirondack Mountain Club (ADK) and subscribing to the *Adirondack Explorer*. Information about both can be found on their websites: ADK.org and AdirondackExplorer.org.

The state Department of Environmental Conservation's emergency hotline is 518-891-0235.

How hard is that hike?

In gauging the difficulty of a hike, two major consid-erations are its length and elevation gain. In our statisti-cal overviews, provided at the head of each chapter, we indicate the distance of the hike (in miles) and the over-all ascent (in feet). These figures are used to calculate the average grade from the trailhead to the summit or high point. As a measure of steepness, the average grade can be misleading if a long, flat approach precedes the ascent. In those cases, we also calculated the grade of just the steep part of the trail. We call this the "climbing grade" (shown in parentheses in the chart below).

The four charts can be used to compare the relative difficulty of the hikes. The last represents our ranking. Though based on the statistical overviews, it is somewhat subjective.

ROUND-TRIP IN MILES

1. Haystack	6.6
2. Scarface	6.4
3. Copperas Pond	4.8
4. Van Hoevenberg	4.4
5. Henry's Woods	3.8
6. Flume Knob	3.4
7. Balanced Rocks	3.2
8. John Brown Farm	2.5
9. Cobble Hill	2.0
10. Mount Jo	2.0
11. Baker	1.6
12. Owl's Head	1.2

ELEVATION GAIN IN FEET

1. Scarface	1,480
2. Haystack	1,240
3. Flume Knob	1,180
4. Baker	860
5. Balanced Rocks	830
6. Van Hoevenberg	740
7. Mount Jo	685
8. Owl's Head	460
9. Henry's Woods	450
10. Cobble Hill	450
11. Copperas Pond	240
12. John Brown Farm	130

Baker Mountain is a short hike, but the trail is rather steep.

AVERAGE GRADE	(%)		OVERALL DIFFICULTY RANKING
1. Baker	20.4		1. Scarface (hardest)
2. Owl's Head	14.5		2. Haystack
3. Flume Knob	13.1	(22.3)	3. Flume Knob
4. Cobble Hill	13.1		4. Balanced Rocks
5. Mount Jo	10.3		5. Van Hoevenberg
6. Balanced Rocks	9.8		6. Henry's Woods
7. Scarface	8.8	(23.7)	7. Baker
8. Haystack	7.1	(21.4)	8. Mount Jo
9. Henry's Woods	6.8		9. Cobble Hill
10. Van Hoevenberg	6.4	(15.0)	10. Owl's Head
11. Copperas Pond	3.9		11. Copperas Pond
12. John Brown Farm	1.8		12. John Brown Farm

1 Cobble Hill

Elevation: 2,331 feet
Distance: 0.65 miles to summit; 2-mile loop
Elevation gain: 450 feet
Average grade: 13.1%
Trailhead coordinates: N 44° 17.637', W 73° 58.293'

Visitors to Lake Placid are often struck by the gorgeous view of the High Peaks from the shores of Mirror Lake. They may not be as impressed with the rocky knob just across the water, but that's no reason to ignore it. This unassuming protuberance, known as Cobble Hill, offers a grand vista of the larger mountains—a nice payoff for a quick hike.

The shortest path to the summit is only 0.65 miles, but it requires you to climb up or scramble around a short but steep slab near the top. Some folks, including young children, might find the exposure intimidating. You can avoid the slab entirely by taking the back trail to the summit. It's longer—1.3 miles—but mellow.

Ideally, you'll combine the trails into a 2-mile loop, ascending by the short route and descending by the long one, which takes you past pretty Echo Lake. That's the hike we'll describe here.

The trail begins at Northwood School, a private boarding school. Although Cobble Hill's summit is in the state-owned Forest Preserve, the trail begins on school property. Please be respectful.

From the parking area, look for a sign on a tree about

The open slab on the hike up Cobble Hill offers outstanding views.

sixty feet to the right. This is where the trail starts. Walk 0.1 miles to a junction, where another sign directs you to go right. You'll encounter a number of trail junctions on this hike, but all are marked by signs.

At 0.25 miles, you reach a four-way junction with an old woods road. This is where the two trails diverge. Hikers ascending by way of Echo Lake should turn left here. Those ascending by way of the slab should cross the road and head uphill.

A short distance from the road, the direct route crosses a wide trail and then bends right to avoid small cliffs. At 0.45 miles, turn left at yet another trail junction. A moment later you find yourself at the base of the slab.

If you are capable and have good rubber on your boots, you can scramble directly up the open rock. If you'd rather stick to the safety of the trees, traverse right and ascend along the edge of the woods. There may be a fixed rope to help you get started.

The views from the top of the slab are almost as good as those from the summit. You can see the village of Lake Placid and countless mountains, including several High Peaks.

Just after the slab, you pass through a narrow slot between boulders and dip slightly to a miniature col within a stand of balsam fir. At 0.65 miles, you come to the junction with the back trail. Bear right to reach the summit less than a minute away.

In the 1950s, investors planned to create a ski area on Cobble Hill; the venture failed, but the chair-lift foundations still exist.

Cobble Hill's ledges offer open views from east to west. Both Mount Marcy and Algonquin Peak, the only two mountains in the state above 5,000 feet, can be seen. Other prominent peaks include the Sentinels, Cascade Peak (with its distinctive "7" scar), Gothics in the Great Range, and Mount Colden with its many slides.

On the way back, turn right at the first junction if you're doing the loop. The trail descends at a moderate grade for a half-mile to Echo Lake. Bear left and walk along the south shore of the pond. Bear left when the trail splits near the end of the pond, then bear right at the next junction. This puts you on the woods road you crossed on the approach. Shortly you arrive back at the four-way intersection. Turn right to return to the trailhead.

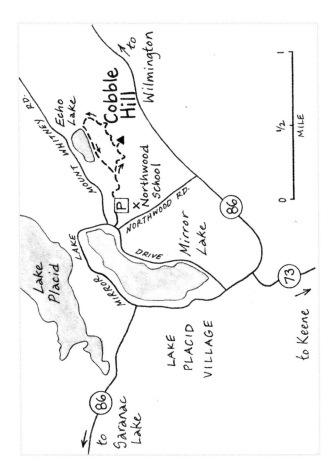

DIRECTIONS: From NY 86 (Main Street) at the north end of downtown in Lake Placid, turn onto Mirror Lake Drive and go 1.1 miles to the rear entrance road for Northwood School on left. Turn and go 0.1 miles to a trailhead parking area on the left. Do not use the school's main entrance off Northwood Road. It doesn't lead to the parking area.

2 Henry's Woods

Elevation: 2,270 feet
Distance: 3.8-mile loop
Elevation gain: 450 feet to Rocky Knob
Average grade: 6.8%
Trailhead coordinates: N 44° 15.801', W 73° 58.900'

The trails at Henry's Woods on the outskirts of Lake Placid were designed to withstand heavy use, and since opening to the public in 2009, they have proved to be popular. Locals visit Henry's Woods often to hike, jog, mountain-bike, and walk their dogs. The trails are suitable for all but the youngest children.

Henry's Woods is not part of the public Forest Preserve. The 212-acre tract is owned by the Henry H. and Marion S. Uihlein Foundation. Among other things, visitors are prohibited from smoking, boozing, picking plants, camping, or listening to music without headphones.

Altogether, there are 4.85 miles of trails. The 0.3-mile Connector Trail and the 2-mile Loop Trail lie at the heart of the network, but the best views are found on two secondary routes: the Rocky Knob Trail and Plateau Trail. The hike we describe connects these four trails.

All outings begin on the Connector Trail. As soon as you enter the woods, you'll see a large kiosk on the left. Stop here to consult the trail map and read the rules. From the kiosk, the Connector goes up an easy grade to a three-way junction with the Loop Trail, which is marked by green disks.

You can go either way on the Loop Trail, but we'll as-

Hikers enjoy a variety of views from the Henry's Woods trails.

sume you turn right and travel counterclockwise. Incidentally, you will have noticed that the Connector and Loop are much wider and smoother than typical hiking trails.

Less than a quarter-mile down the Loop, you'll pass the Switchback Trail on the left. This is a short trail (0.25 miles), marked by blue disks, that zigzags up a steep slope to the Plateau Trail. (The Switchback is the only trail not included in this hike.) In another 0.2 miles, you come to the Bridge to Nowhere, a small wooden suspension bridge that leads to a platform next to a rock wall. It's a nifty bridge, but its purpose is mysterious.

In another tenth of a mile, you come to the Rocky Knob Trail on the right. Marked by red disks, this 0.9-

mile route exemplifies modern trail design. In the Adirondacks, trails seem in a hurry to get to the summit: they tend to go straight up, which leads to erosion and tired legs. The Rocky Knob Trail, in contrast, winds gently back and forth through a hardwood forest as it climbs to a pair of lookouts.

At 0.4 miles from the Loop Trail, you arrive at a junction maybe forty feet below the summit of Rocky Knob. Bear right for the first lookout, which offers a view of Lake Placid and Whiteface, the fifth-highest mountain in the Adirondacks. Then return to the junction and take the other fork to a ledge with a view of the Great Range in the High Peaks Wilderness. Cross the ledge and follow the trail down the other side of Rocky Knob to rejoin the Loop Trail.

> The trails at Henry's Woods were designed by Tony Goodwin, the longtime editor of the Adirondack Mountain Club's guidebook to the High Peaks region.

Turn right and follow the Loop Trail uphill a short distance. Just as it starts to level, you pass a bench. In another 0.2 miles, you reach the Plateau Trail. Turn left. Marked by yellow disks, this trail stays level except for tiny dips. Soon after passing the upper end of the Switchback Trail you come to two views, the first of the Sentinel Range east of Lake Placid, the second of Wilmington Notch. After 0.9 miles, the Plateau Trail rejoins the Loop Trail. Turn left to go downhill to the three-way junction with the Connector Trail and then bear right to get back to your starting point.

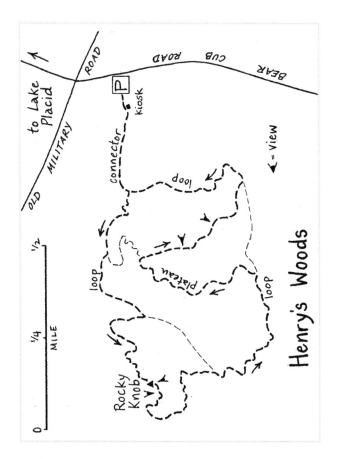

DIRECTIONS: From the junction of NY 73 and NY 86 in Lake Placid, head south on NY 73. After 1.5 miles, just before the Olympic ski jumps, turn right onto John Brown Road and then immediately take another right onto Old Military Road. Go 0.75 miles and turn left onto Bear Cub Lane. The entrance to Henry's Woods is on the right in less than a tenth of a mile.

3 John Brown Farm

Elevation: 2,010 feet
Distance: 2.5-mile loop
Elevation gain: 130 feet
Average grade: 1.8%
Trailhead coordinates: N 44° 15.240', W 73° 58.313'

This is the easiest and most unusual trip in the book: a hike through history as well as the woods, affording an opportunity to visit the grave and farm of John Brown, the militant abolitionist who led the raid on a federal arsenal in Harpers Ferry, West Virginia, in 1859.

The state Office of Parks, Recreation, and Historic Preservation manages the farm and small cemetery, which are open to the public May through October (except Tuesdays). Even when they're closed, you are free to hike the trails anytime during daylight hours.

> Russell Banks, an author with a home in Keene, wrote an acclaimed novel about John Brown called *Cloudsplitter.*

Located just outside Lake Placid, the property has several trails. The hike we describe takes you in a loop through fields and forest and past the farm. Except for one short climb, you'll be walking on the flats or downhill. Because the trail junctions are unmarked, you must pay close attention to the directions.

The trail starts at a field on John Brown Farm Road, about a tenth of a mile before the farm itself. From the parking area, a sign directs you to the left, but before set-

John Brown's nineteenth-century farm is a state historical site.

ting off, check out the nearby interpretive sign to learn a bit about John Brown.

The field offers a splendid view of the High Peaks to the south, including the two tallest, Mount Marcy and Algonquin Peak. The McKenzie Range can be seen to the northwest. Follow the well-worn path a short distance to a split, then bear left. Soon you enter a forest of pine, spruce, and balsam fir.

At 0.3 miles, you come to a junction near the ski jumps built for the 1980 Winter Olympics. Turn right to follow a wide trail down a corridor of evergreens. Stay on this trail until reaching John Brown's farmhouse (just past the caretaker's home) at 0.75 miles. The trail turns left here, next to a register, but before continuing, you'll probably want to spend time at the graveyard and the farmhouse.

After the raid at Harpers Ferry, Brown was tried and

hanged. His wife, Mary, brought his body to the farm to be buried. Eleven of his co-conspirators, including two of his sons (both killed in the raid), also are buried here. Some of Brown's saga can be gleaned from interpretive signs outside the cemetery.

John Brown, circa 1856

To continue the hike, return to the register. Just after passing an old barn, bear left. The trail curves around the edge of a small field and comes to a gate, where it begins climbing moderately for about 0.15 miles. Partway up the hill, bear right at a junction.

Once the grade eases, the trail remains level as you pass through a mixed forest. At 1.25 miles, you pass another gate. You are now on private property, so stay on the trail. Just after the gate, bear right at a junction. The trail parallels a field and begins a gradual descent. It levels again, crosses a woods road, and comes to another field. At 1.7 miles, you begin a steeper descent.

At the bottom of the hill, bear right at a junction. After crossing another road, you come to a gate at 2.1 miles and are back on public land. A quarter-mile past this gate, turn left at a junction. At 2.5 miles, you leave the woods and enter a field with a view of Whiteface Mountain and the Sentinel Range to the northeast. Cross the field to return to the parking area.

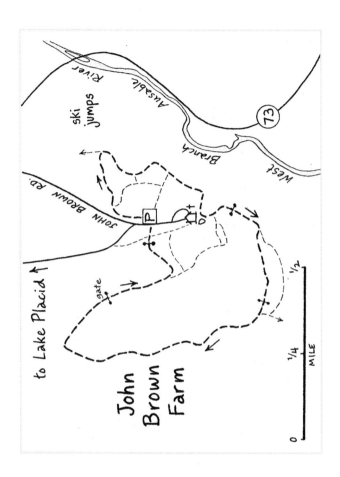

DIRECTIONS: From the junction of NY 73 and NY 86 in Lake Placid, drive south on NY 73 for 1.5 miles to John Brown Farm Road. Bear right and go 0.6 miles to a parking area on the left, a tenth of a mile before John Brown's farmhouse.

4 Haystack Mountain

Elevation: 2,787 feet
Distance: 3.3 miles to summit
Elevation gain: 1,240 feet
Average grade: 7.1%
Climbing grade: 21.4%
Trailhead coordinates: N 44° 17.558', W 074° 03.059'

Haystack Mountain is not Mount Haystack, the third-tallest mountain in the Adirondacks, but it does reward the hiker with excellent views. From its summit, you can see most of the High Peaks as well as much more. And it's a lot easier to get to than the other Haystack.

Although it's 3.3 miles to the summit, getting to the top requires less than a mile of real climbing. Over the last 0.75 miles, you gain more than 800 feet. Parts of the trail may be too steep for young children.

If doing Haystack, you may run into hikers working on the Saranac Lake 6. Marked by blue disks, the trail begins on the north side of Route 86 between Lake Placid and Saranac Lake. After leaving the register, you rock-hop across a small stream and ascend a gentle slope through a forest of pine and hemlock. The forest soon changes to hardwoods, which are more typical of this trail.

At 0.5 miles, the trail crosses a larger stream. In another mile, after small ups and downs, you arrive at a bedrock outcrop in a small opening in the forest. There are very limited views to the west and southwest.

You now descend to a broad but shallow stream, crossed

Big Burn Mountain lies across the valley from Haystack.

on planks. The trail becomes noticeably wider as it merges with a former woods road. At 2.2 miles, you pass a foundation on the right. The trail climbs at an easy grade along Little Ray Brook and shortly reaches a junction. The way right (marked by red disks) leads to McKenzie Mountain, tallest of the Saranac Lake 6. Bear left to go to Haystack.

In less than a tenth of a mile, you come to a spillway dam on Little Ray Brook. You can cross the brook by tiptoeing across the dam or rock-hopping below it. Once safely across, be prepared for strenuous climbing. Although the trail is steep and often eroded, it eases off in places to allow you to catch your breath.

Just below the summit, you reach a lookout on the right with views of Lower Saranac Lake, Oseetah Lake, Scarface Mountain in the foreground, and the High Peaks in the distance. This is just a taste of what lies ahead.

The trail ends at a clearing of grasses, shrubs, and bedrock slabs with a 270-degree vista. If you walk (carefully) down the sloping slabs, you can see Whiteface Mountain to the northeast, about eight miles away. Other prominent High Peaks include Giant, Gothics, Marcy, Colden, Algonquin, Nye (recognized by its slide), the Sewards, and the Santanonis. Directly across the valley is Big Burn Mountain. Scarface, another of the Saranac Lake 6, lies almost due south.

> The spillway dam on Little Ray Brook was built to create a water supply for a state prison in Ray Brook.

Most people will return by simply turning around, but those on the 6er quest may want to knock off Haystack in tandem with McKenzie. To do this, go to the end of the clearing, veer left into the woods, and look for an unmarked path. Follow the path about a half-mile downhill to the Jackrabbit Ski Trail. (If you lose the path, walk generally northeast). Turn right at the Jackrabbit and follow it a half-mile or so to a trail junction. Turn left to go to McKenzie. The summit is 1.7 miles away. Some hikers may prefer to do the peaks in reverse order since the herd path to Haystack's summit is not as steep as the marked trail. There may be a cairn on the Jackrabbit marking the start of the path.

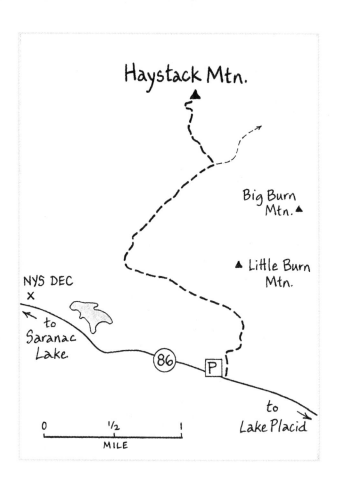

DIRECTIONS: From Lake Placid, drive west on NY 86. About a mile from town you'll pass Old Military Road on the left. At 1.3 miles beyond this junction, you'll see a large pullout on the right. Park here.

5 Scarface Mountain

Elevation: 3,088 feet
Distance: 3.2 miles to lookout
Elevation gain: 1,480 feet
Average grade: 8.8%
Climbing grade: 23.7%
Trailhead coordinates: N 44° 17.875', W 74° 05.004'

Scarface takes its name from the prominent patch of bedrock on its northwest face, visible from the village of Saranac Lake. Despite the unappealing appellation, the hike up Scarface has much to offer, including an easy stroll through beautiful pine woods and unique views of Oseetah Lake, the Sawtooth Range, and the western High Peaks.

As in the case of Haystack Mountain, the trail to Scarface is fairly level for more than two miles, after which the climbing begins. In the hardest section, you must scramble up a short but steep band of bedrock, which can be wet and slippery. This may be too difficult or scary for young children—or even some adults. However, you can assist yourself by grabbing tree roots.

> The wooden bridge that crosses Ray Brook was built by a prison work crew from Camp Gabriels in 1985.

The trailhead is in Ray Brook, a hamlet between Lake Placid and Saranac Lake. At the outset, you walk through a pine forest whose soft duff is easy on the feet. At 0.2 miles, the trail comes to train tracks used by the Adirondack Scenic Railroad, a tourist train. After crossing the tracks, you

Hikers cross Ray Brook on a sturdy wooden bridge.

pass through another pine forest and, in a quarter-mile, descend to Ray Brook (the stream) where it winds through an alder swamp.

The stream is crossed on a large wooden footbridge. It's a good place for taking photos of the brook and the north ridge of Scarface. On the other side of the brook, the trail climbs a short distance and then levels. In a few places, a small increase in elevation results in a change of forest from evergreen to hardwoods. At 1.6 miles, the trail skirts a clearing with concrete slabs from an old homestead.

Less than a quarter-mile past the clearing, you come to a T-intersection. A small sign indicates that you should turn left here. Shortly after the turn, the trail crosses a stream and soon begins to steepen. At 3.0 miles, you reach the

The Scarface ledges offer vistas in several directions.

small cliff band. Scramble up or around it as best you can. Just beyond you encounter more exposed bedrock, but the climbing is easier, ending on a ledge with views of waters and mountains to the west and north.

Turn right to follow the trail a bit farther to the main lookout at 3.2 miles. Many mountains in the High Peaks Wilderness can be seen from here, including Street, Nye, Henderson, Ampersand, the Sewards, and the Sawtooth Mountains. Oseetah Lake lies to the west less than three miles away.

Most people turn around at the lookout ledge, but the actual summit is a half-mile away and can be reached by following an unmaintained path. Although Scarface is one of the Saranac Lake 6, the rules of that quest do not require you to continue to the viewless summit.

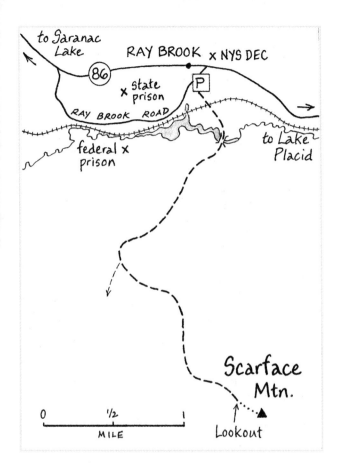

DIRECTIONS: From Lake Placid, drive west on NY 86 about four miles. When you reach Ray Brook, you will see on the right the entrance to the Adirondack Park Agency and state Department of Environmental Conservation. Just beyond this, turn left onto Ray Brook Road. The trailhead parking area will be on the left 0.1 miles after the turn.

6 Baker Mountain

Elevation: 2,452 feet
Distance: 0.8 miles to summit
Elevation gain: 860 feet
Average grade: 20.4%
Trailhead coordinates: N 44° 19.903', W 74° 06.926'

Situated on the edge of Saranac Lake village, Baker Mountain is a favorite hike of local residents, but it also sees a fair amount of tourist traffic, more so since the advent of the Saranac Lake 6 challenge in 2013. The summit offers a knockout view of McKenzie Mountain, with the High Peaks in the distance.

Given its popularity, Baker has a number of trails and herd paths, yet the official trail, marked by red disks, is well-trodden and easy to follow.

One of the rock-climbing routes on Baker's cliffs is called TB or Not TB, a reference to Saranac Lake's history of treating tuberculosis patients.

The trail begins at a DEC sign across the road from Moody Pond. Shortly after signing in at the register, you come to a trail junction. Either way will get you to the summit, but bear right to stay on the marked trail. You can hike in a loop by returning on the other trail.

At first, the trail is wide as it follows an old woods road that once served a quarry. The ascent is steady, but not overly steep. After 0.4 miles, the trail levels for a spell, then resumes climbing through a pine forest, often on outcrops of bedrock.

A hiker relaxes on one of Baker's many open ledges.

Following a steep pitch, you may notice a secondary trail leading left. This is a more direct route to the top, but bear right to keep on the official trail, which soon emerges onto bedrock ledges with spectacular views in three directions. Splayed out below are Lower Saranac Lake, Lake Flower, and Kiwassa Lake. Scarface Mountain and Haystack Mountain—two of the other peaks in this book—are just a few miles away. Farther off are bigger mountains, including the Sawtooth Range and the High Peaks. While ascending the ledges, parents will want to keep an eye on young children.

If you can tear yourself away from the vista, veer left and follow the trail a short distance to the top. A National Geodetic Survey disk marks the true summit. Nearby is a ledge with a splendid view of McKenzie Pond (once a water source for the village), the McKenzie Range, Haystack

Part of the trail passes through a forest of red pine.

Mountain, and many of the High Peaks, including Mount Marcy, the highest of the high. There is another ledge, to the left of the first, with a view of the Saranac River valley.

To return to the trailhead, you can retrace your steps or descend by the back trail. Though unmarked, the alternative route is easy to find and follow. You will see it on the left a few feet beyond the survey disk. Shortly after beginning the descent, look for a side path on the left that leads to a ledge with a view of the village and Lower Saranac Lake.

The upper part of the back trail is steep in places and often rocky, but it eventually mellows. After about 0.4 miles of descent, you may notice a path on the right. This leads to lookouts above some rock-climbing cliffs. Beyond this junction, it's an easy walk out to the road.

The round-trip hike on the official trail is about 1.6 miles. Doing the loop is only slightly longer.

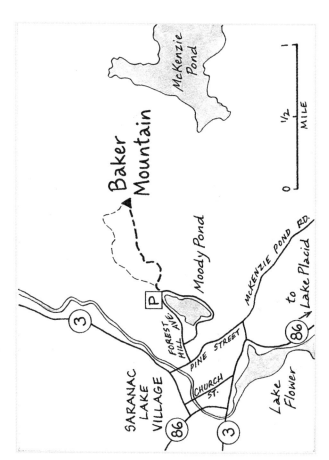

DIRECTIONS: From Lake Placid, take NY 86 to Saranac Lake. Once in the village, turn right onto Brandy Brook Avenue (where NY 86 bends 90 degrees to the left) and drive 0.1 miles to its end. Turn left onto Pine Street and go 0.4 miles, taking the first right onto Forest Hill Avenue. Follow this street 0.5 miles to the north end of Moody Pond. The trailhead is on the left.

7 Mount Van Hoevenberg

Elevation: 2,860 feet
Distance: 2.2 miles to summit
Elevation gain: 740 feet
Average grade: 6.4%
Climbing grade: 15%
Trailhead coordinates: N 44° 11.627', W 73° 57.044'

When the photographer Carl Heilman II created a poster titled "The High Peaks Wilderness," he chose as his subject the vista from Mount Van Hoevenberg. It was a good choice.

Van Hoevenberg sits on the northern edge of the High Peaks Wilderness, affording a spectacular view of the big guys. Heilman's poster identifies 15 High Peaks, and that's only a partial list of those that can be seen.

> Van Hoevenberg is a homocline, a mountain whose bedrock strata dip in one direction. The tilt accounts for its steep scarp.

The trail from Meadows Lane is marked by blue disks. Although it's 2.2 miles to the summit, the first mile or so is nearly flat. On this part of the route, the forest alternates between red pine and hardwoods. The pine forest is especially attractive.

At 0.9 miles, you come to a large beaver pond filled with snags, skeletal trees that died when the beavers flooded the land. The trail turns left to skirt the pond. As you walk along the shore, check out the large beaver dam. If you look across the water to the northeast, you can see your

Many of the High Peaks are visible from Van Hoevenberg's ledges.

destination—the summit ledges of Van Hoevenberg.

The trail on the other side of the pond is often very muddy. To keep your boots dry, chances are you'll have to hop on boulders and tiptoe across logs and narrow planks. Once it pulls away from the pond, the trail dries out as it rises gently. At a bit over a mile, the trail dips to cross a stream and then begins ascending the mountain.

The trail cuts across the mountain through open hardwoods. Although the climb is steady, it isn't overly hard. The trail steepens a bit as you pass some small cliffs on the left, reached at 1.5 miles, but it then eases, allowing you to relax before the final ascent.

As you near the top, the forest changes to red spruce and balsam fir, with some white birch thrown in. These species

PHOTO BY NANCIE BATTAGLIA

The trail skirts a beaver pond before climbing to the summit.

are well adapted to the wind and cold encountered on the summit.

Emerging onto the first ledge, you find yourself staring at Mount Marcy, Mount Colden, and Algonquin Peak, with South Meadow in the foreground. You also can see the beaver pond you passed on the way in. Don't linger too long: the trail continues to two other ledges over the next tenth of a mile. The last affords the best view of the dramatic north face of Gothics—with its vast expanse of bare rock—and other peaks in the Great Range.

Bring a map and compass and spend some time identifying the many peaks that lie before you.

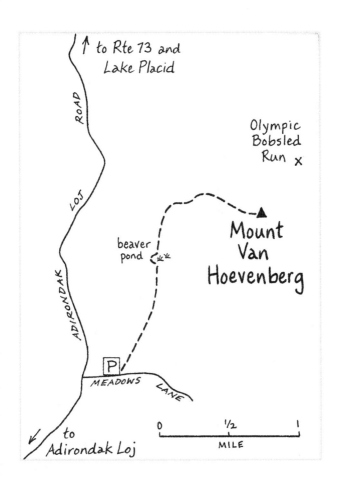

DIRECTIONS: From Lake Placid, drive south on NY 73 to Adirondak Loj Road on the right, which starts next to a vast field with an iconic view of the High Peaks. Take the Loj Road for 3.8 miles to Meadows Lane. Turn left and drive 0.2 miles to the trailhead on the left.

8 **Mount Jo**

Elevation: 2,876 feet
Distance: 2-mile loop
Elevation gain: 685 feet
Average grade: 10.3% (via Long Trail)
Trailhead coordinates: N 44° 10.972', W 73° 57.815'

Mount Jo is one of the most beloved small peaks in the region, because of its views of the High Peaks, its proximity to Adirondak Loj, and its romantic history.

Henry Van Hoevenberg, the founder of the original Adirondack Lodge, named the 2,876-foot mountain after his fiancée, Josephine Scofield, who disappeared while visiting Niagara Falls in 1877. Mount Jo overlooks Heart Lake, also named by Van Hoevenberg.

The Adirondack Mountain Club owns a square mile around Heart Lake, including Mount Jo.

From Adirondak Loj (the phonetic spelling was adopted later), it's a short climb to the summit and a spectacular vista. Those not staying at the lodge should begin the hike at the nearby High Peaks Information Center, where the Adirondack Mountain Club (ADK) maintains a public parking lot. If you don't belong to ADK, the parking fee is $10 per car.

Two routes—the Long Trail and the Short Trail—lead to the summit. We will describe a clockwise loop hike that ascends by the Long Trail and descends by the steeper Short

Algonquin Peak looms over the summit of Mount Jo.

Trail. Of course, you are free to do the loop in the opposite direction. Both trails are well-worn and often rocky.

On the drive in, you pass a ticket booth just before the High Peaks Information Center. After parking, walk back to the booth and look for a trail on the far side of the road. This is the start of the hike.

The trail curves through a stand of balsam fir and reaches a junction at 0.15 miles with a trail from Adirondak Loj. Turning right, you pass a cabin that houses a nature museum and shortly come to another junction. Turning right again, you come to the Mount Jo register and a colorful interpretive sign.

You now begin climbing, but the grade soon eases as

the trail bends west and contours along the slope. You should be able to glimpse Algonquin Peak and Heart Lake through the trees.

At 0.4 miles, the trail splits. Go straight (bearing left) to ascend via the Long Trail, which is easier on the knees. The trail climbs in spurts, reaching a junction with the Rock Garden Trail at 0.85 miles. Going straight here, you pass a twenty-foot-high rock wall on the right. After this, the trail steepens and stays steep for a good distance.

At 1.1 miles, the Short Trail comes in from the right. Go straight. The trail next winds past a rocky knob (don't mistake it for the top) and clambers over bedrock to the summit ledge at 1.25 miles.

The view takes in numerous High Peaks, but most prominent are Wright and Algonquin almost due south, looming over Heart Lake. Mount Marcy, the state's highest peak, lies to the southeast. Between Marcy and Algonquin is the slide-scarred Mount Colden. The rocky cap of Cascade Mountain can be seen to the east. If you turn around and look through the trees, you also may be able to spot Whiteface Mountain to northeast.

To descend, return to the last junction and turn left for the Short Trail. The steep descent is aided by stone steps built by ADK's trail crew. You will pass some lookouts on the way down.

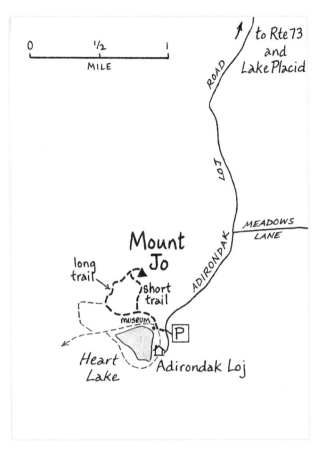

DIRECTIONS: From the junction of NY 73 and NY 86 in Lake Placid, drive south on NY 73 for 3.4 miles to Adirondak Loj Road on the right (1.4 miles after crossing the Ausable River). Turn and drive 4.7 miles to the Adirondack Mountain Club ticket booth. Just past the booth, turn left to park at the High Peaks Information Center. The club charges a fee for parking. If no one is in the booth, you can pay in the information center.

9 Balanced Rocks

Elevation: 2,995 feet
Distance: 1.6 miles to lookout
Elevation gain: 830 feet
Average grade: 9.8%
Trailhead coordinates: N 44° 13.134', W 73° 53.257'

Pitchoff Mountain is a long rocky ridge with outstanding views of the High Peaks. You can hike the entire ridge in a 3.8-mile traverse over several summits, but you also can find good views in a much shorter hike to Balanced Rocks on a large wide-open ledge.

The Pitchoff trail begins across Route 73 from the trailhead for Cascade Mountain, perhaps the most frequently climbed of the High Peaks. Marked by red disks, the trail ascends gradually through a hardwood forest. Not far from the start, you may see yellow blazes on some trees marking the boundary between the Forest Preserve and private property.

> A tenth of a mile down the road from the trailhead is Stagecoach Rock, a boulder etching that commemorates an earlier era of transportation.

At 0.2 miles, the trail turns northeast away from the private land. It's easy hiking over the next half-mile, with gradual uphills and small dips. After entering a stand of red spruce and balsam fir, the trail reaches a lookout at 0.6 miles. A ledge to the right offers a close view of Upper Cascade Lake and Cascade Mountain.

The highest mountain on the horizon is 5,114-foot Algonquin Peak.

You come to a second lookout at 0.75 miles. From this ledge, again just off the trail, you look directly across the valley at Cascade's long bedrock scar, which was lengthened and widened during Tropical Storm Irene in 2012. You also can see a few more High Peaks, including Wright, Colden, and Marcy.

Soon you come to a short, steep section that leads to more lookouts along the trail. You also can glimpse a rocky knob looming ahead—your destination. At one mile, you descend briefly to a col, after which the climbing gets harder. As soon as you leave the col, you climb beside a slide path. You may need to grab roots and rocks to help you ascend. At the top, the trail turns left and levels as it curls

PHOTO BY NANCIE BATTAGLIA

Cascade Mountain is a prominent landmark on the hike to Balanced Rocks.

around the back of the mountain.

At 1.2 miles, the trail starts to climb again, sometimes steeply. In another quarter-mile, you reach a junction with a "View" sign nailed to a tree. The through trail bears left to climb to the 3,600-foot summit of Pitchoff, but you want to turn right. Shortly after the turn you come to another junction. The short path on the left leads to a view. To reach Balanced Rocks, bear right and follow the trail to a broad ledge with views to the east, south, and west. You can see many High Peaks besides Cascade, including Big Slide, Mount Marcy, Mount Colden, and Algonquin Peak. Behind you is the summit of Pitchoff. Near the end of the ledge are the Balanced Rocks, large boulders left behind by the retreating glaciers thousands of years ago.

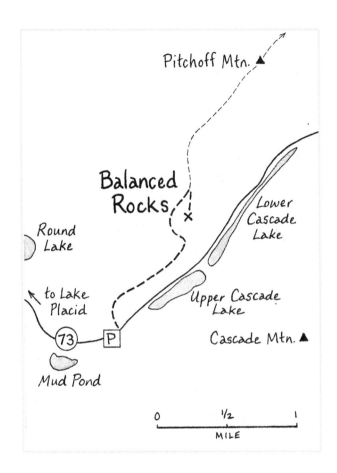

DIRECTIONS: From Lake Placid, drive south on NY 73. At 6.0 miles past the Olympic ski jumps, pull into a parking area on the right. The Pitchoff trail begins a hundred feet away on the other side of the road. Note: there is a spillover parking area shortly before this one.

10 Owl's Head Mountain

Elevation: 2,120 feet
Distance: 0.6 miles to summit
Elevation gain: 460 feet
Average grade: 14.5%
Trailhead coordinates: N 44° 14.864', W 73° 49.832'

Owl's Head is a short hike with numerous lookouts, making it a favorite of young families or anyone with an hour to kill. There are cliffs along the trail and on the summit, so parents will need to keep an eye on children.

> There are three other Owl Heads in the Adirondacks with hiking trails. The next closest is Owl Head Lookout in Elizabethtown.

Although the summit is in the public Forest Preserve, the trail starts on private land. The climbing begins at once and the vistas soon follow. At 0.15 miles you come to the first lookout: a ledge with a view to the southwest of Cascade Mountain, one of the High Peaks, and the rocky humps of Pitchoff Mountain.

After 0.25 miles, the trail skirts a small cliff and reaches another lookout with a similar but more expansive view. Bear left for easy hiking along a narrow ridge. At 0.4 miles, after the trail steepens again, you enter the Forest Preserve. Beyond here the views are almost continuous the rest of the way to the summit.

At 0.5 miles, the trail levels briefly. Toward the right is a nearly vertical rock wall with several technical climbing

PHOTO BY NANCIE BATTAGLIA

Owl's Head offers hikers a big reward for small effort.

The peak is a favorite among families with young children.

routes. Often rock climbers scale the wall after setting up top ropes on the Owl's Head summit.

On the final scramble to the top, you are treated to a view in a different direction—to the north toward the end of Pitchoff and neighboring Brown Mountain.

On the summit, the main ledge offers views to the west and southwest. Except for Route 73 running between Cascade and Pitchoff, you see few signs of civilization. Another prominent ledge offers a southeast-to-southwest vista that includes Hurricane Mountain (with its fire tower), Baxter Mountain, Giant Mountain, Round Mountain, and Porter Mountain.

If you hunt around among the scrubby pines, you can find views in virtually all directions, and in late summer you might find some blueberries as well.

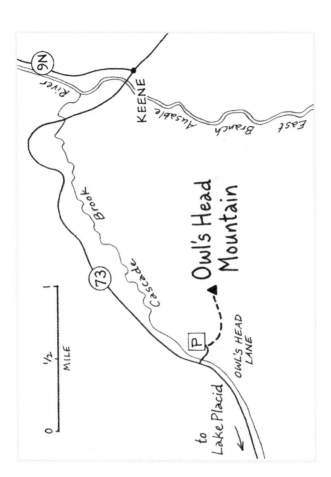

DIRECTIONS: From Lake Placid drive south on NY 73. At 7.9 miles past Adirondak Loj Road (with its expansive view of the High Peaks), look for Owl's Head Lane on the right. Turn here and go 0.3 miles, then turn left and park. The trail is on the right.

11 Owen, Copperas, and Winch Ponds

Elevation: 1,864 feet
Distance: Up to 4.8 miles round-trip
Elevation gain: 240 feet
Average grade: 3.9%
Trailhead coordinates: N 44° 19.548', W 73° 54.645'

If you (or your children) aren't up for climbing a mountain, you might enjoy an easy hike through the woods to visit these three ponds east of Lake Placid. Although you're never far from the road, the terrain blocks the traffic noise so you feel like you're in the wilderness.

> The lean-to at Copperas Pond is the only lean-to in the 24,000-acre Sentinel Range Wilderness.

There are two trailheads. We'll describe a round-trip that begins at the Owen Pond trailhead, the one closer to Lake Placid. If you visit all three ponds as well as the lean-to on Copperas's north shore, you'll hike nearly 4.8 miles, but shorter variations are possible.

If you have a second car, you could do a through trip, finishing at the Copperas Pond trailhead. This would cut the hiking distance to 3.5 miles, but the trail descending from Copperas to the highway is steep and rocky.

From the Owen Pond register, you ascend gradually for a tenth of a mile and then descend to the pond's outlet. The trail (marked by blue disks) climbs briefly along the brook, passing among hemlocks, before descending again

Don't forget to look before you leap.

to Owen Pond at 0.6 miles.

Look for a herd path leading to the pond's cedar-lined shore. From the water's edge, you have a view of the Sentinel Range. To the southeast is a bedrock slide on an unnamed peak near Kilburn Mountain. The slide was created when a rainstorm washed away vegetation in 1995.

After following the pond's north shore, the trail veers left and goes over a small hill, reaching a stand of dead trees at 0.85 miles. Listen and look for woodpeckers here.

The steepest part of the trail lies just ahead: you climb about 120 feet in 0.2 miles. At the height of land, you may be able to see Whiteface Mountain, the fifth-highest peak in the Adirondacks, through the trees. A short descent brings you to the southwest corner of Copperas Pond.

Shortly, you come to the pond's outlet where an opening in the large hemlocks provides a spectacular view of Whiteface. This is the scenic highlight of the hike.

Soon after crossing the outlet, you come to an unmarked junction. Bear right, following yellow disks, to go to Winch Pond a half-mile away. This trail begins with a short climb, then descends to another junction. The way left leads to the highway. Bear right to reach Winch Pond in a tenth of a mile. Water lilies decorate the little pond. There are many dead trees in the shallow water near the shore, a sign of beaver flooding. Of the three ponds, Winch offers the least-inspiring views.

Return to Copperas Pond. If you want to visit the lean-to, a quarter-mile away, turn right when you reach the blue-marked trail. The trail skirts the water and soon reaches a junction. The way right leads to the second trailhead. Bear left to reach the lean-to in a tenth of a mile. The site offers a nice view of 3,892-foot Kilburn Mountain to the southeast.

If you skip the lean-to, your round-trip will be only 4.25 miles. If go to the lean-to but skip Winch Pond, your hike will be 3.75 miles. If you want an even shorter hike, you could turn around at the Whiteface view. Your round-trip then would be just 2.65 miles.

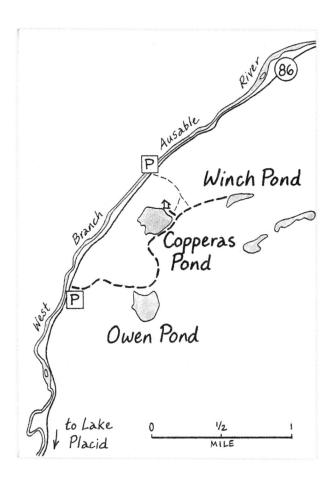

DIRECTIONS: From the junction of NY 73 and NY 86 in Lake Placid, drive east on NY 86 for 5.5 miles to the Owen Pond trailhead on the right. The Copperas Pond trailhead is 0.9 miles farther down the road. Parking for that trailhead is on the opposite side of the road.

12 Flume Knob

Elevation: 2,270 feet
Distance: 1.7 miles to summit
Elevation gain: 1,180 feet
Average grade: 13.1%
Climbing grade: 22.3%
Trailhead coordinates: N 44° 21.969', W 74° 50.470'

Flume Knob offers a vista far different from the others in the book: looking down the Ausable River valley, you can see part of Lake Champlain and, on the horizon, the Green Mountains of Vermont. The first half of the hike is easy, but it gets steep at the end.

> The popular Flume swimming hole is across the highway and a bit downriver from the Flume Trails parking area.

The knob gets its name from the Flume, where the West Branch of the Ausable squeezes through a narrow rock canyon. The Flume Trails, where the hike begins, are a network of mountain-bike routes, and on the return you can alter your route for variety.

On the way to Flume Knob you pass numerous trail junctions and so must be careful not to take a wrong turn. You won't get lost if you remember to always follow blue disks and, for the first half-mile, to stay on the wide Corridor Trail.

From the register, walk thirty yards or so to a junction and turn right onto the Corridor Trail. It climbs briefly,

A hiker takes in the view from Flume Knob.

then levels. Shortly, you come to the first of a series of junctions, marked by signs that indicate the direction of the Corridor Trail and/or the way to Flume Knob.

At 0.5 miles, the Corridor Trail takes a sharp left, but you want to continue straight. You are now on the Upper Connector Trail, which links the Flume Trails to the Whiteface Mountain Ski Area. In a tenth of a mile, the trail, now narrower, bends left and soon begins a gradual but steady climb.

You reach a major junction at 0.9 miles. Bear right to leave the Upper Connector and continue a steady ascent. Over the next 0.8 miles, you'll climb nearly nine hundred feet—one of the tougher workouts in the book.

At 1.2 miles, the trail turns right, indicated by an arrow. After this, the climbing becomes steeper. At one point, you clamber through a slot in a rock wall. During the ascent, you enjoy partial views of the valley and mountains.

PHOTO BY NANCIE BATTAGLIA

Paper birch can be found along most Adirondack trails.

After a brief level stretch, the trail switchbacks up a piney slope to gain the spine of a ridge. Follow the ridge for the last few hundred yards to Flume Knob.

The spacious ledge offers views in three directions. Lake Champlain and the Green Mountains lie toward the east. The rocky ridge of the Jay Range stands out in the southeast. Giant Mountain can be seen more to the south over the shoulder of the Sentinel Range, the massive range in the foreground. Looming above Flume Knob, just to the north, is Marble Mountain.

On the return trip, retrace your steps as far as the Corridor Trail. Instead of going straight (the way you came in), turn right here. The trail descends briefly and passes a junction with the Lower Connector Trail. Just past here, bear right onto the Bluff Trail, which is marked by red disks. Follow this along the edge of a low bluff and beaver meadow for 0.4 miles. When you reach the Corridor Trail again, turn right to reach the parking area. You are almost there.

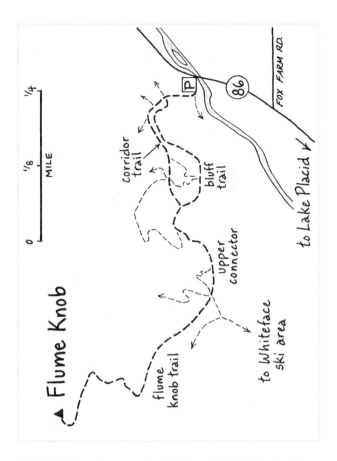

DIRECTIONS: From the intersection of NY 73 and NY 86 in Lake Placid, drive east on NY 86 for 10.3 miles to the Flume Trails parking area on the left, reached immediately after crossing the Ausable River.

The Saranac Lake 6

In 2013, the village of Saranac Lake started offering commemorative patches to hikers who climbed six mountains located within a short driving distance of the community. The program proved to be popular from the get-go. In the first year, more than five hundred hikers qualified. They also earned the right to ring the 6er Bell at Berkeley Green in the heart of the village.

If you climb the Saranac Lake 6, you can obtain your patch and a sticker by sending the following information to the village, along with a $10 check (your name will be added to the 6er roster):

- Date you climbed each of the six mountains.
- The time you reached the summit of the last mountain.
- Your mailing and email addresses.

The information should be mailed to Village of Saranac Lake, Saranac Lake 6ers, 39 Main St., Saranac Lake, NY 12983.

Three of the Saranac Lake 6 are among the twelve hikes selected for this book: Baker, Scarface, and Haystack. The other three mountains—McKenzie, Ampersand, and St.

Regis—were either too big or too far from Lake Placid to make the cut. However, in this section of the book, we offer a brief overview of these three hikes for the benefit of aspiring 6ers.

The Saranac Lake program is modeled on the Adirondack 46ers, a nonprofit group that offers patches to hikers who climb the forty-six High Peaks (most of which top 4,000 feet).

For more information, visit saranaclake6er.com.

McKenzie Mountain

Elevation: 3,861 feet
Distance: 5.3 miles to summit
Elevation gain: 2,221 feet
Average grade: 7.9%
Trailhead coordinates: N 44° 17.558', W 074° 03.059'

At 3,861 feet, McKenzie Mountain is the hardest of the Saranac Lake 6, but it offers great views of Lake Placid and numerous mountains, including the High Peaks. If you start at Route 86, you can climb Haystack Mountain on the way and thus knock off two of the Saranac Lake 6 in one hike (see the Haystack chapter for details).

From Route 86, follow the Haystack trail for 2.4 miles (mostly flat), then bear right at a junction. At 3.6 miles you cross the Jackrabbit Ski Trail. From here, it's 1.7 miles to the summit, with very steep climbing in places. On the summit there are lookout ledges on both sides of the trail.

You can shorten the hike by starting at Whiteface Inn Road in Lake Placid and going up the Jackrabbit Trail for 1.9 miles to the aforementioned intersection, then turning right onto the McKenzie trail. The round-trip is 7.2 miles instead of 10.6 miles.

DIRECTIONS: From Lake Placid, drive west on NY 86. About a mile from town you'll pass Old Military Road on the left. At 1.3 miles beyond this junction, you'll see a large pullout on the right. Park here.
If opting for the shorter route, drive 1.4 miles down Whiteface Inn Road from NY 86 in Lake Placid to the Jackrabbit Trail on the left.

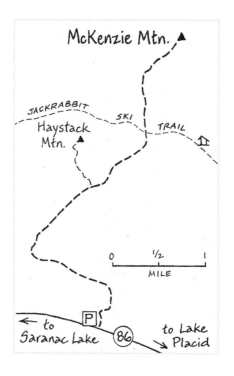

Ampersand Mountain

Elevation: 3,352 feet   **Distance:** 2.7 miles to summit
Elevation gain: 1,175 feet   **Average grade:** 8.2%
Trailhead coordinates: N 44° 15.089′, W 74° 14.375′

Ampersand Mountain's bald summit offers striking vistas of both the High Peaks and the Saranac Lakes. Marked by red disks, the trail starts out flat as it passes through an impressive old forest. At 1.2 miles, the climbing begins. You reach the former site of a fire observer's cabin at 1.7 miles. Beyond, the trail steepens considerably. At 2.4 miles, the trail eases and winds past rock formations before emerging onto the bald summit. A plaque honors Walter Channing Rice, who served as an observer from 1915 to 1923.

DIRECTIONS: From the intersection of Main Street and NY 3 in Saranac Lake (near town hall), drive 8.2 miles west on NY 3 to a parking lot on the right. The Ampersand trail begins across the road. Another trail leads from the lot to a beach on Middle Saranac Lake, a good place to swim after the climb.

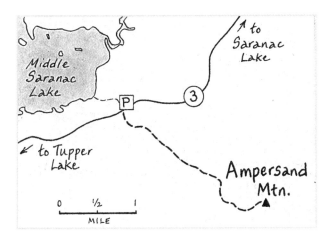

St. Regis Mountain

Elevation: 2,874 feet   **Distance:** 3.3 miles to summit
Elevation gain: 1,266 feet   **Average grade:** 7.3%
Trailhead coordinates: N 44° 25.928', W 74°18.013'

St. Regis Mountain has outstanding views of the ponds in the St. Regis Canoe Area as well as large lakes, with the High Peaks on the horizon. From the parking area walk down a dead-end road 0.1 miles to the trail register on the right. The first few miles of the trail, which is marked by red disks, are easy. After crossing a stream on a wooden bridge, the trail begins a gradual climb. The climb gets steeper near the top. A fire tower still stands on the summit, though it is no longer used.

DIRECTIONS: From Saranac Lake, take NY 86 north to Paul Smiths. Turn right, then make an immediate left onto Keese Mills Road. Go 2.5 miles to parking area on the left.

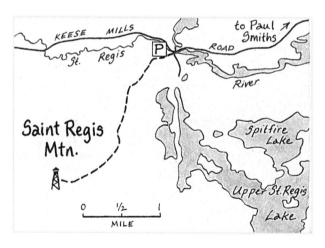

Adirondack Guidebooks from
Lost Pond Press

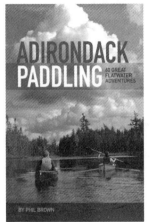

Adirondack Paddling
60 Great Flatwater Adventures

Phil Brown, editor of the *Adirondack Explorer*, describes 60 flatwater paddling trips. Full-color maps and photos.

Adirondack Birding
60 Great Places to Find Birds

John M.C. Peterson and Gary N. Lee reveal the best places for finding the species coveted by birders. Color photos by Jeff Nadler.

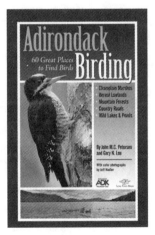

Both guidebooks can be purchased in stores or online from the Adirondack Mountain Club. **www.adk.org**

View the full Lost Pond catalog on our website. **www.LostPondPress.com**

EXPLORE
the Adirondacks
Subscribe now and enjoy year-round adventures

THE ADIRONDACK EXPLORER:

7 issues a year packed with hikes, paddles, ski treks, climbs, birding, wildlife plus all the information you need to stay on top of the issues that shape this great Park.

Subscribers enjoy free access to the Adventure Planner, an online collection of hundreds of excursion stories complete with photos, maps and directions.

Visit AdirondackExplorer.org for more info.
Or call 1-888-888-4970.